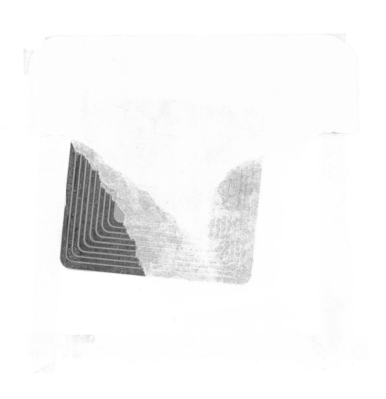

POUCHES, PADS, AND Plumes

Lynn M. Stone

Rourke
Publishing LLC
Vero Beach, Florida 32964

www.rourkepublishing.com

PHOTO CREDITS: © Lynn Stone: title page, page 4, 5, 6, 9, 11, 12, 13, 15, 16, 17, 19, 21; © zimmytws: page 7; © Damir Spanic: page 8; © Suzann Julien: page 10; © Clay Greene: page 14; © Kitch Bain: page 18; © Michael Zurawski: page 20

Editor: Meg Greve

Cover design by: Nicola Stratford, bdpublishing.com

Interior design by: Renee Brady

Library of Congress Cataloging-in-Publication Data

Stone, Lynn M.

Pouches, pads, and plumes / Lynn M. Stone.
    p. cm. -- (What animals wear)
 Includes index.
 ISBN: 978-1-60472-310-6 (hardcover)
 ISBN: 978-1-60472-788-3 (softcover)
 1. Body covering (Anatomy)--Miscellanea--Juvenile literature. I. Title.
 QL942.S758 2009
 590--dc22

                  2008012970

Printed in the USA

CG/CG

Table of Contents

Pouches

Animal **pouches** have many purposes. The mother kangaroo's pouch is a home for her baby, known as a joey.

A joey stays in its mother's pouch until it is several months old.

5

Some birds have pouches along their throat and lower beak. The soft, thin skin of the pouch helps a bird to release heat.

The pelican's pouch stretches like a balloon. It serves as a fish net.

Pads

Many animals have **pads** on the bottom of their feet. Cats, dogs, and bears are some of the mammals who have pads.

Pads help protect a wolf's feet and quiet its footsteps.

9

Pads are plump and soft. Tough, bare skin covers animal pads.

The tiger's pads are the largest of any cat.

Plumes

Plumes are long, fancy feathers. Some species of birds grow plumes used for courtship.

The male peacock spreads its plumes into a tail fan of feathers.

13

During courtship, birds show off their plumes. Plumes help birds such as **herons** and **egrets** attract others of their kind.

The egret's lacy plumes help it find a mate.

15

Plates

Plates are sections of hard, tough material. Some animal plates cover soft skin. Some act as an animal's skin.

The armadillo has bands, or plates, to protect its body.

Some rhinos appear to wear plates of armor. In fact, their thick skin is not in sections. It just grows in folds.

A rhino looks like an armor-plated tank, but its skin is quite sensitive to sun and insect bites.

Pouches, pads, plumes, and plates are all very different. Each helps animals to survive.

The male prairie chicken attracts a mate by filling its throat pouch with air to make a booming sound.

Glossary

egrets (EE-grits): tall wading birds with long, sharp beaks

herons (HER-ons): wading birds who are close cousins to egrets

pads (PADS): soft areas covered with tough skin on the bottom of some animals' feet

plates (PLAYTS): hard coverings similar to nail or bone on certain animals

plumes (PLOOMS): long, fluffy feathers found on many birds

pouches (POUCH-ez): growths on certain mammals, birds, and fish that look like bags

Index

Further Reading

Pohl, Kathleen. *Peacocks*. Gareth Stevens Audio, 2007.

Townsend, Emily Rose. *Armadillos*. Coughlan Publishing, 2003.

Wood, Jeremy. *I Wonder Why Kangaroos Have Pouches and Other Questions about Baby Animals*. Houghton-Mifflin, 2003.

Websites

www.kidsplanet.org/factsheets/kangaroo.html
www.mbgnet.net/fresh/lakes/animals/pelican.html
www.sandiegozoo.org

About the Author

Lynn M. Stone is a widely-published wildlife and domestic animal photographer and the author of more than 500 children's books. His book *Box Turtles* was chosen as an Outstanding Science Trade Book and Selectors' Choice for 2008 by the Science Committee of the National Science Teachers' Association and the Children's Book Council.